T0381384

Memories of
ENGLAND

by Lily Ann Graff

To order additional copies of this book, contact:
Xlibris
844-714-8691
www.Xlibris.com
Orders@Xlibris.com

ISBN: Softcover   978-1-4568-6525-2

Library of Congress Control Number: 2011901951

Print information available on the last page

Rev. date: 09/28/2020

Memories of

ENGLAND

by Lily Ann Graff

NEW BEGINNING

Away from the country where I was born

Away from the usual familiar ways

Away from the loves ones that I adored.

It all happened on the 19th day

In the month of February.

The year is too long ago

When life was sweet and promises were kept

When all my heart and desires of a future were but too perfect.

The day was then, a new beginning in a foreign place,

But not so that my spirit would reject.

Eighteen months in the land of my ancestors

I did embrace, the chance to discover

New but old ways.

And all my senses came to be one

My response was a newness to my soul,

Beautifully fresh, clean and sound.

THE BLUE BIKE

The wheels are turning,

At a steady pace they ride

Trying to safely arrive

To a destination of warmth.

The rain falls cold and covers

The young woman's green coat.

The long wavy hair becomes

With each stroke of the wheel

A stream of water flowing

From every golden strand.

Shivering and in a puddle

She arrives to the house

On Frederick Road.

RED PANELLED WINDOWS

Long days, steady rain,

Grey days that don't end.

Window panes all in red

And a young woman

All amazed!

In the house full of tenants,

Anything goes.

Friends and friends of theirs,

Come and go.

But in one downstairs bedroom,

Only order, goodness and faith

Is what reigns!

Kneeling on the floor

Morning and night she prays

As a gentle sense of protection

Overtakes her and her own.

And day after day

The steady rain, the grey day

And the long day

Will continue

As the young woman

Looks through the red window panes

Of the house she calls her own.

MARYLEBONE

A train leaving from Marylebone station in London departs promptly. It is not a
new train, but has the old flavor of one built back in the fifties. The

seats are small but cushioned and there is a thrill in the air of the unknown.
Traveling north from London to a destination in Buckinghamshire. The

ride is steady, not too fast not too slow. Making its stops in every little village on
its way to Aylesbury. Passing through Harrow-on-the-Hill, Rickmansworth,

Chorleywood, Chafont/Latimer, Amersham, Great Missenden, Wendover, Stoke
and Mandeville. This makes the ride almost double the time, but going

through the towns brings to my mind a certain nostalgic charm of Britain's past.

I, sitting in my small soft seat, cherish the scenes of rolling green hills, canals and
market squares as I savor a small chocolate biscuit.

Exhibition Organ

Long pipes, thin, silvery and shiny,

The sound is large, brave and mighty.

Organ pedals that with the push

Sound out so grave and fine.

The protagonist on Exhibition

Road is the organ.

Solemn sounds come through its doors.

Mixture of clarinets, trumpets

Violas and flutes.

Very few people know

The feeling of pedals sliding down

This organ's keyboard,

And the trembling that goes through.

For one moment I am the One

The only One that through strikes

Of keys and pedals produces the

Joy of the King of all sounds.

Grand it is and the Joy is full.

This one Cemetery

On a Tuesday morning
In the month of May
She strolls down a cementary
Like any other day.

The tombs of stone lay flat,
And moss grows on every corner
Of this green and grayish scene.

Not a sound is heard,
Not a cry of grief and dismay,
Nature itself is present
As the tombs lay and lay.

She stops in front of a grave
The name too familiar and fine.
Almost two hundred years have gone by,
And then a chill runs down her spine.

In loving memory of
Lillian Margaret,
Beloved wife of Joseph Langstone
Who died at the age of 24
On the 26th of May 1807.
Aylesbury, Buckinghamshire.

She shares her same name
And almost her same age,
Dreams and plans of two,
Two young ladies, 21 and 24,
Can come to an unexpected end
When life is but too beautiful
And exciting to ignore.

In her mind she reads:
In loving memory of
Lily Ann Margaret
Beloved girlfriend of Peter
Who died at the age of 21
On this month of May of 1980.
Aylesbury, Buckinghamshire.

All in all, it is felt at that moment,
That life is an experience of learning,
Sharing, and giving of oneself,
Nothing is wasted and all will return.

FOG

A night in the cold, damp fall of Britain's past

I walked the narrow paths of pebbled streets,

Wet, slippery and steep.

As the fog takes me, so thick,

So dense and mysterious.

The darkness of the night happens,

As the moon becomes black

With the ambiance of the fog,

And with fear becoming me.

As the deserted streets come by

I run down as quickly as I can

To a more familiar place.

Where a room and a bed

Will secure me for the night.

A CHRISTMAS NOTE

A cold frosty morning,

The hills of Guildford

Awake to a Christmas.

So many Christmases

Have gone by

With the listening

Of bells from churches

That stand high

In their stones,

Beautiful and cold.

I, alone standing

In the icy pavement

Of Nightingale road,

Listening to the bells.

Alone and silently

Enjoying the whole scene.

A scene too perfect to describe.

How I wished

You were there,

My love, but alone

I took it all, silently, perfectly, calm.

A SUNDAY MORNING RIDE

Circling around narrow roads,

Down and up hills.

From Guilford to Godalming

In a dense forest of leaves.

Circling round and round

The pedals go, first fast then slow,

As they make their way

Up the steeps of this country scene.

Little glimpses of sunrays seep through the trees

Making the cold brisk morning wind not so cold.

The air brings at times a smell of burning wood,

Wood coming through the brick chimneys

Of the scared houses throughout the road.

Memories of a young girl

Enjoying her weekly Sunday ride.

The day is now,

The memories where then.

RED DOUBLE DECKER BUS

Up and down
The red double decker bus
Goes and goes
Through narrow streets,
And jerks at all its stops,
Making people look for
A pole to grip on tight.

She is watching
From the very front seat
Of the upper floor.
Number 23 of London's bus transit.

Sitting close, her hand feeling his hand,
As smiles and laughter are exchanged
And the amusement of riding
Without a destination fills the air.

Streets go by and more and more
They become unfamiliar,
But she feels protected and warm.

His hand still holding hers
Assuring her he is there.

The night is cold and wet,
She, wearing a funny hat.
He wearing a plaid shirt.
Together enjoying the ride
From the top of a red double decker bus.

Row houses upon row houses go by,
The busy streets and shops
Make their way to little parks.
Soon the artificial lights
Become natural light from the moon.

Streets are calm
And few people walk by
As her hand is lifted up,
And in a sweeping mood
She is taken down
And off the red double decker bus.

A TORCH

One torch lights up the darkness,

The darkness is big, heavy but calm.

We are in the Moorlands,

Where meadows of the color lilac overflow.

Just north of York, not far from the Northern Sea,

I walk slowly with the torch,

As it shines down a pathway of gold.

The little cottages and old stables

Stand side by side as they go.

One of them is my little home,

A home full of hope for a future,

Love and a feeling of belonging,

Nothing matters more.

My heart is full and I am here to stay

In the vast Moorlands of today.

BRITISH FOOD

Flapjacks, caramel chocolate squares, ginger malt bread, Christmas pudding,
minced meat pies and gooseberry ones in hot custard are just a few of

Britain's favorites. But I must not forget the wonderful trifles prepared each
Sunday by lovely families that would have us for dinner.

Food, I adore food, but only the exquisite, well done. Yes, you must let
yourselves be a little hungry to get the full effect.

THE RED TELEPHONE BOOTH

A red telephone booth
Stands near the Thames
On the end of old Putney bridge.
Each night at ten
It's heavy iron door opens
To receive the daily visit
Of an energetic 22 year old.
She will call and report
The daily numbers
She is to record.
Eight hours of proselyting
Four discussions in Hammersmith
Five street approaches
And one person committed to baptism.
Day after day she will keep
A detailed log of her endeavors
And the red telephone booth
Will be her connection
To the other world.
As she speaks out her numbers
She looks out into the Thames.
The water is black but it shines
With the reflection of the moon
And the metal railing of old Putney bridge.

CARLISLE

Little villages, surrounded by rolling hills,

So green they can be seen through the fog.

Sheep throughout, scatter the scene,

White, bucolic and tender.

Solace it brings to the sight.

Family of mine that inhabited these lands,

Wool collectors and fabric makers.

Together they stood, loved and fought

Together they worked, grieved and died.

Standing here, by the Hadrian Wall

I can feel their sorrows

And the endurance they lived,

Even when beauty embraces my eyes.

THE LANDLADY

She was not a little lady

But she was not a big lady either

Her name was Vera.

She was a landlady 30 years ago

In her little row house of Putney.

Today she came to my mind.

She was at least seventy then.

Life is short, but for some it might be long.

The thought of Vera dead

Caused me to be sad.

For although I did not know her very well

She was my landlady for six long months.

Today, thirty years later, and in London

I cannot see her for she is gone.

TATE GALLERY

Bright red, bold yellow

Blue and green forever.

Shadows of beautiful grey,

Pure whites and classic creams.

All of them you will find

In an array of lines, figures

And marvelous displays of what can only be called GRAND.

The Tate gallery.

STERLING CASTLE

High you stand overlooking the town,

The valleys, the meadows and streams.

Strong and steady you withheld your enemies.

And through the centuries, even today,

On a cold but bright morning

You look overpowering

Engaging and frightful.

CLIFFS OF DOVER

On a white cliff

Standing tall and still

In front of a foreign country

I await the time

For you to come.

Together the start of a new life,

It will be you and me alone.

Printed in the United States
By Bookmasters